T0008897

THE SECRET LIFE OF THE
CHUPACABRA

Published by Capstone Press, an imprint of Capstone
1710 Roe Crest Drive, North Mankato, Minnesota 56003
capstonepub.com

Library of Congress Cataloging-in-Publication Data is available on the Library of
Congress website.

ISBN: 9781669004059 (hardcover)
ISBN: 9781669040415 (paperback)
ISBN: 9781669004011 (ebook PDF)

Summary: Readers take a look into the secret life of the chupacabra to uncover
surprising facts, including the cryptid's first appearance, its favorite meal, and more.

Editorial Credits
Editor: Abby Huff; Designer: Heidi Thompson; Media Researcher: Jo Miller;
Production Specialist: Tori Abraham

Image Credits
Alamy: Matthew Corrigan, 13 (chupacabra); Associated Press: Eric Gay, 28; Capstone:
Matthew Stevens, 5, 9, 11, 15; Science Source: Jaime Chirinos, 17; Shutterstock:
cynoclub, 6, Daniel Eskridge, 19, delcarmat, Cover (chupacabra), 7, 22, 27, Jeffrey
Schwartz, 14, kersonyanovicha, 25, LynxVector, 22 (hat, mittens, scarf), Makkuro
GL, 29 (mask), Maria Spb, 21 (chupacabra), Mr. SUTTIPON YAKHAM, 7 (wings), 13,
mrkob, 20, Paolo Trovo, 12, Pascale Gueret, 26, Potapov Alexander, 29 (chupacabra),
Radu Bercan, 23, worapatpong rattanapan, 21 (teddy bear), Yevhenii Chulovskyi, 22
(alpine scene), Yurlick, Cover (cone)

Design Elements
Shutterstock: Kues, ONYXprj, Studio77 FX vector

All internet sites appearing in back matter were available and accurate when this
book was sent to press.

Printed and bound in China. PO5132

TABLE OF CONTENTS

Words in **bold** are in the glossary.

MEET THE CHUPACABRA

The chupacabra is a master of **disguise**. Some people say it looks like an alien. Others say it's like a hairless dog or large bat. Does the chupacabra enjoy playing dress-up? No matter what, it always drinks the same thing. It slurps blood! Uncover more about this sneaky **cryptid**.

FACT

Science hasn't shown that cryptids are real. But many people believe they are.

WHAT'S GOT YOUR GOAT?

Are you the champion of all things chupacabra? Do you know the cryptid's:

1. Height?

2. Wingspan?

3. Eye color?

4. Favorite meal?

BONUS: What grows down the beast's back?

Baa! Let's get out of here!

ANSWERS

1. 4 to 5 feet

2. 8 to 10 feet

3. Red, black, or gray

4. Goats

BONUS: Spikes or quills

ONE SHY CRYPTID

No one keeps a secret like shy chupacabras. They stayed hidden until 1995. That year, Madelyne Tolentino saw a figure outside her home in Puerto Rico. But she wasn't having anyone over. Who could it be?

A strange animal stood near the house. It was about 4 feet tall. It moved on two legs. It had gray eyes and long arms. Spikes lined its back. Madelyne screamed, and the creature hopped away. Maybe the chupacabra just wanted to visit?

FACT

Madelyne saw a movie about aliens before the sighting. How she described the cryptid closely matched the look of the movie aliens.

STYLE SWITCH

The chupacabra enjoys changing up its style. In many sightings, people say it's like a dog with no hair. It walks on four legs. A long **snout** and sharp **fangs** complete the look.

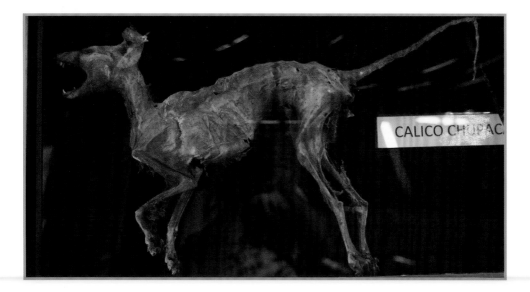

In other reports, the chupacabra flies with bat-like wings. It flicks out a forked tongue.

WHAT'S FOR DINNER?

Move over, Dracula. There's a new **vampire** in town. The chupacabra has a gross diet. It sucks blood!

But not just any red stuff will do. This cryptid feeds on farm animals. Its strong sense of smell helps it track down dinner.

SNIFF

SNIFF

SNIFF

SNEAKY EATER

The chupacabra drinks the blood of sheep, pigs, and cows. But what treat is on top of its list? Goats!

The chupacabra sneaks onto farms. It feeds on many animals in a flash. It slurps down its big meal. Then it runs off before it can get caught.

FACT

Chupacabra means "goat-sucker" in Spanish.

HOW TO BE A CHUPACABRA

Being a chupacabra isn't easy. It follows a set of rules:

- Stay out of the spotlight.
  Come out at night.

- No talking allowed.
  Make a hissing sound instead.

- Spray a gross smell if people get close.
  Then run away.

Chupacabras have likes and dislikes.
They can't stand bright lights. Headlights or
a flashlight will send them running.

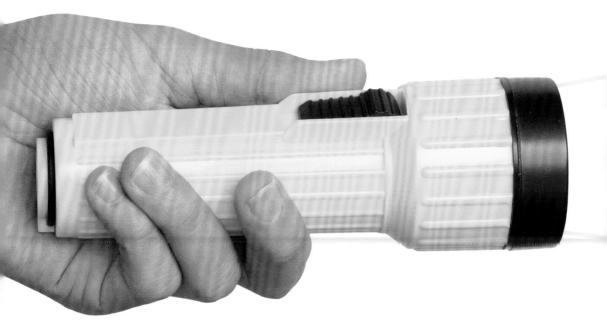

But they do like toys. One **witness** said a chupacabra reached into her open window. It stole her teddy bear!

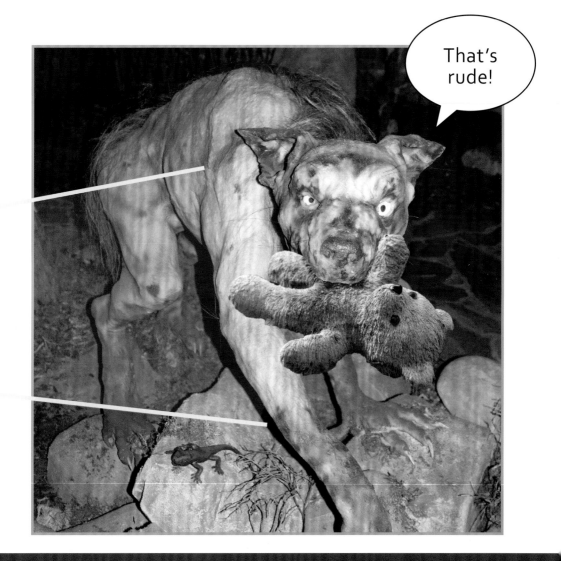

That's rude!

WORLD TRAVELERS

Chupacabras can live almost anywhere. They like warm places best. They enjoy the heat of South America. They like the southern United States too. But they have been spotted in colder places. The chupacabra has even popped up in China and Russia.

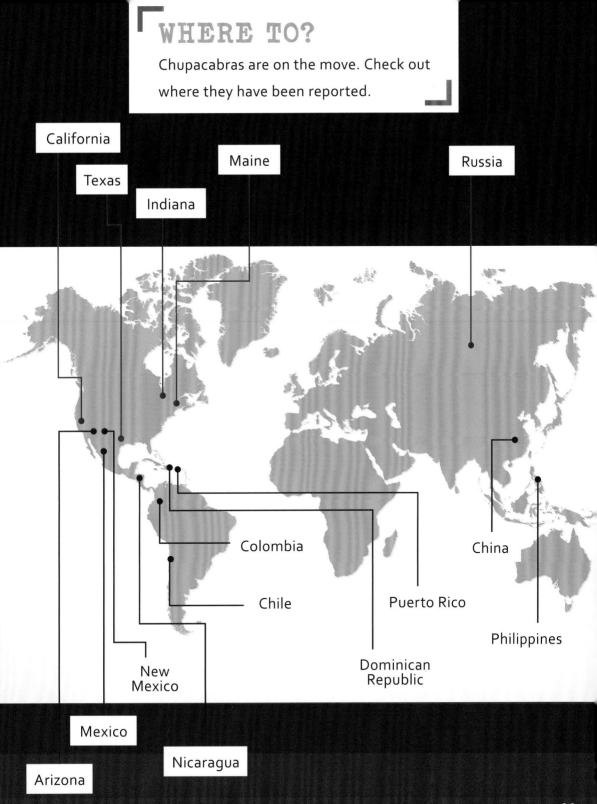

WHERE TO?

Chupacabras are on the move. Check out where they have been reported.

California

Texas

Indiana

Maine

Russia

Colombia

Chile

China

Puerto Rico

Philippines

New Mexico

Dominican Republic

Mexico

Nicaragua

Arizona

MYSTERY SOLVED?

Chupacabras may not win any beauty contests. But what are they, exactly? Some people say chupacabras are aliens. Witnesses have seen gray, hairless creatures with dark eyes near **UFOs**. Sound familiar?

Others think the cryptids come from our own planet. They say the U.S. government made chupacabras in labs!

Sit, Fido! Chupacabras might be related to pet dogs. Some scientists say the cryptid is a coyote. The animal just has a skin problem called **mange**. Mange causes fur to fall out. It can also make the skin look dry and crusty.

FAMOUS PHOTO

In 2007, Phylis Canion found a dead creature near her Texas ranch. The thing had grayish-blue skin. Sharp teeth filled its mouth. Phylis said it was a chupacabra. The photo she snapped became famous.

07/14/2007

Did she finally uncover the secret of the chupacabra?

GLOSSARY

cryptid (KRYP-tid)—an animal that has not been proven to be real by science

disguise (dis-GAHYZ)—the act of changing your looks in order to hide or not be recognized

fang (FANG)—a long pointed tooth

mange (MEYNJ)—a skin disease caused by mites that leads to itching, hair loss, and scabby skin

snout (SNOWT)—the long front part of an animal's head that includes the nose, mouth, and jaw

UFO—an object in the sky thought to be a spaceship from another planet; UFO is short for Unidentified Flying Object

vampire (VAM-pahyur)—from stories, a thing that drinks blood from the living

witness (WIT-niss)—a person who has seen or heard something

READ MORE

Finn, Peter. *Do Monsters Exist?* New York: Gareth Stevens Publishing, 2023.

Krensky, Stephen. *The Book of Mythical Beasts & Magical Creatures.* New York: DK Publishing, 2020.

Troupe, Thomas Kingsley. *Searching for Chupacabra.* Mankato, MN: Black Rabbit Books, 2021.

INTERNET SITES

How Stuff Works: Hunting Bigfoot and Other Beasts
science.howstuffworks.com/science-vs-myth/strange-creatures/cryptozoology.htm

International Cryptozoology Museum
cryptozoologymuseum.com

Wonderopolis: What Is El Chupacabra?
wonderopolis.org/wonder/what-is-el-chupacabra

INDEX

ABOUT THE AUTHOR

Megan Cooley Peterson has been an avid reader and writer since she was a little girl. She has written nonfiction children's books about topics ranging from urban legends to gross animal facts. She lives in Minnesota with her husband, daughter, and cuddly kitty.